The Unofficial Guide to Wirecast

BY PAUL RICHARDS

ISBN: 9798590559633

The Unofficial Guide to Wirecast

DEDICATION

Dedicated to my countless StreamGeek friends and colleagues.

CONTENTS

ACKNOWLEDGMENTS

Stephen Heywood, Lynn Elliot, and everyone else at Telestream who helped create the outline for this book.

FORWARD

Live streaming has come a LONG way.

Wirecast initially launched in 2004 with the value proposition to help *anyone* make live streams that looked like TV broadcasts. Wirecast was ahead of its time in many ways. Think about it: That was before Facebook Live. Before YouTube Live…. Heck, some people were still using dial-up modems to connect to the Internet! But our developers (who are still with the company to this day) saw the future. And the future was live video that anyone could produce and stream, right from their own computers.

Today, almost 17 years later, Wirecast's mission remains **to make high quality live production available to the masses.** Now, though, we all have a lot more tools, platforms, equipment, processing power and bandwidth to draw from.

This makes producing live streams even more exciting and creative!

Although the COVID-related shutdowns this past year have been extremely challenging for most of us in many ways, I have been inspired by the resilience and resourcefulness of people as they have found ways to keep their businesses going and remain connected to their communities. Live streaming has been a big part of that, as people have successfully shifted their live events online.

From churches streaming their services so their members could stay safe at home; to corporations keeping their businesses going with live streamed meetings, product launches and events; and even non-profit and event companies broadcasting their traditionally-live concerts and fundraisers to fully-online audiences – it has been a year where the ability to produce quality live streams has become an essential part of our lives.

As we move forward in 2021, and even as the world starts opening up to in-person events, I expect that live streaming has reached a critical mass. It may not ever fully replace in-person events, but it plays an important role that will need to be considered for every live event moving forward.

It's not just about staying connected and expanding your audience anymore. It also represents new revenue stream opportunities, as well as the potential for massive cost savings. Every meeting, tradeshow, concert, sporting event, lecture, marketing event, (and much more) should be planned with consideration for how live streaming that event can improve or enhance the outcomes in a variety of ways.

I want to thank Paul Richards for writing *The Unofficial Guide to Wirecast*. This Guide is a comprehensive, easy-to-follow resource for using Wirecast. As an experienced streamer, Paul gives an excellent overview of how to get started, as well as how to use some of the advanced features of Wirecast.

As we move forward and expand the usage of live streaming even more, I hope Wirecast and this Guide can lead the way.

Happy Streaming!

Lynn Elliott
Senior Product Manager, Telestream Wirecast

1 AN INTRODUCTION TO WIRECAST

Wirecast is one of the top live streaming and video production software solutions available today. The software was initially released in 2004 and it has been updated over the years to meet the needs of modern video production. Wirecast is maintained and developed by it's parent company Telestream, which is headquartered in Nevada City, California, USA. The software is available for both Mac and Windows operating systems.

Today, there are more options than ever for video production, live streaming, and recording. They range from inexpensive software packages to professional studios costing tens of thousands of dollars. For those on a tight budget or simply looking for a highly flexible solution, a software solution like Wirecast is a great option. Within the wide range of software options, Wirecast has become one of the best professional-grade options with a price point within the reach of many users. While there are plenty of other options, including OBS (Open Broadcaster Software), xSplit, and eCamm Live, you have likely found that Wirecast standouts for its stability, reliability, and ease of use.

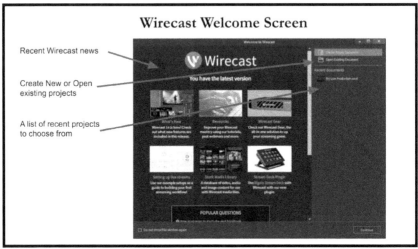

(Wirecast Welcome Screen opens at startup)

What is Wirecast?

Wirecast is designed specifically for creating professional video productions for a wide variety of applications. Most people use the application to live stream or record videos for viewers on online platforms such as YouTube and Facebook. Others use Wirecast for advanced video productions that leverage NDI video connectivity to power monitors with video distributed throughout large campus facilities. Wirecast can be described as a full-featured software-based video switcher.

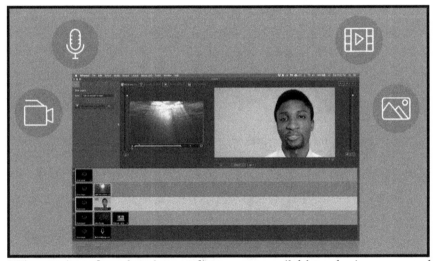

(Wirecast interface showing media sources available to be incorporated into a production)

Wirecast allows for real-time switching between live video cameras and sources such as videos, presentations, remote callers and capture cards. The application includes a powerful audio mixer with professional features that can be used to mix together audio from microphones, videos, and other sources. The software runs on both PC and Mac. The recommended requirements include a 6th generation Intel quad-core i7 at 2.8GHz, for Windows (Windows 10) or macOS (Mojave, Catalina, or Big Sur) using 16GB of RAM, and 500GB solid-state storage.

As with any high-performance software, it is crucial to ensure that you have the hardware capabilities to handle the hardware-intensive functions of manipulating video, encoding, and recording. You can see the full technical specifications at http://www.telestream.net/wirecast/tech-specs.htm.

What Is This Guide Going to Cover?

This guide will detail everything you need to know to download, setup, and start using Wirecast for live streaming and recording. It will cover all of the basics, and go into some of the more advanced options to fine-tune your experience. This book will help you take full advantage of some of the best features of Wirecast. You can start by getting the software up and running, exploring the interface, and understanding the main functions. Next, you will walk through getting all of your cameras and other sources set up. Here you will learn "Wirecast Terminology" for getting shots and layers ready for production. After that, you will learn each major area of Wirecast in a logical order. This will eventually include more advanced features and options like chroma, luma, and color keys, replay, ISO, hotkeys, and social media tools.

How Does Wirecast Compare to Other Solutions in the Market?

There have never been so many options for computer-based live video production software you can run on your very own computer. In fact, there are even cloud-based video production solutions you use with low monthly payments. In the midst of a crowded marketplace, Wirecast has found a space and become quite popular with professionals and hobbyists looking for a more professional option. It is not the least expensive option on the market but the investment is well worth it in the long run for many people. A significant amount of time can be invested in learning a given software solution and many users seek a solution that they can grow into with professional features they can learn to use. Wirecast is available in two versions, the studio version, which is $599, and the pro version, which is $799. You will learn the differences in the next chapter.

With either version, you get an unlimited number of inputs, up to 4K resolution, and unlimited outputs. You can also take advantage of Wirecast Rendezvous to include up to two remote guests in your production and gain access to an integrated stock media library ready to customize for your production. Wirecast is a robust platform and contains all the features and functionality needed by most users looking for a computer-based production solution that can grow with their capabilities over time.

2 GETTING STARTED WITH WIRECAST

Wirecast comes in two different versions. Wirecast Studio is generally suitable for most users. The Wirecast Pro version offers a few more options that are necessary for specific applications that you may find useful. The lower-priced ($599) Wirecast Studio version comes standard with unlimited inputs. This includes an unlimited number of inputs from sources such as video, audio, screen capture, USB, capture cards, NDI, iOS, IP, and web stream sources. This version can handle video up to 4096 x 3072 for production and encoding. It also comes with integrated text, titles, chroma key, built-in and custom transitions, an advanced audio mixer, social media integration, and a stock media library.

Wirecast Studio ($599	Wirecast Pro ($799)
Unlimited Capture • Unlimited inputs • 2 remote guests via Wirecast Rendezvous conferencing	Includes all features of Wirecast Studio, plus:
Enhanced Production • 4096 x 3072 maximum project and encoding resolution • 5 Master Mixing layers • Integrated text, titles, Chroma Key and built-in transitions • Custom transitions, playlists • Advanced audio mixer • Social media integration • Integrated Stock Media	**Advanced Unlimited Capture** • 7 remote guests via Wirecast Rendezvous conferencing

Library	
Unlimited Destination Outputs • Unlimited output destinations + multiple simultaneous record-to-disks • Virtual camera and microphone output • 1-4 slot multi-viewer output	**Advanced Production** • PTZ Camera Control • Pro Audio FX • Sports Production (instant replay, scoreboards) • Virtual Sets and backgrounds
Support Free Email Support & upgrades for a year with Standard Support.	**Advanced Unlimited Destination Outputs** • Adds baseband SDI/HDMI output, NDI program out • 1-17 slot multi-viewer output • ISO Record of individual sources • Multi-track audio recording
	Support Free Email Support & upgrades for a year with Standard Support.
*Pricing & Features Are Subject to Change.	

Wirecast Studio ($599) offers unlimited output destinations, including native integrations designed for an easy login experience with Facebook, YouTube, and Twitter directly through the platform. You can also live stream to any RTMP destination with the custom address.

When you are live streaming you can also record to your harddrive simultaneously. This is ideal for recording your production in a high quality format while live streaming in a compressed format for transport over the public internet. The multi-viewer feature is an output option available to show between 2 and 4 views on an external screen. Wirecast Rendezvous is included in this version allowing you to add two remote guests to your production at any time.

Wirecast Pro ($799) includes all of the same features as the Studio version with several enhancements. You can control PTZ cameras from within the production software in the Pro version allowing you to instantly move cameras by clicking visual thumbnails of camera locations. This edition also adds pro audio effects, sports production plus features like instant replay and scoreboards. Wirecast Pro also includes access to virtual sets and backgrounds. Output capabilities are also expanded with NDI program output, ISO recording of individual sources, and multi-track audio recording. The multi-view output also expands to a total of 17 possible views. Finally,
the Wirecast Rendezvous feature expands to allow up to 7 remote guests.

Both packages come with free standard email support and upgrades to the latest version for one year. After one year, the support service can be extended, including free upgrades for $99 a year. Premium support is also available for $299 a year. This provides access to phone support and remote access services that allows a technician to identify and resolve issues remotely.

Wirecast also offers a wide variety of self-service support, including an extensive knowledge base, documentation, video demos, tutorials, and webinars.

To download Wirecast, just head
to https://www.telestream.net/wirecast/, download the correct version for your computer (PC or Mac) and follow the instructions and prompts. Once the software is installed, you can enter your license key (if you have purchased it already) or use the free trial. The free trial gives you access to a full-featured version of Wirecast with a watermark

on your output. This allows you to try out all the aspects of the software if you are still not ready to make a purchase decision.

3 WIRECAST INTERFACE OVERVIEW

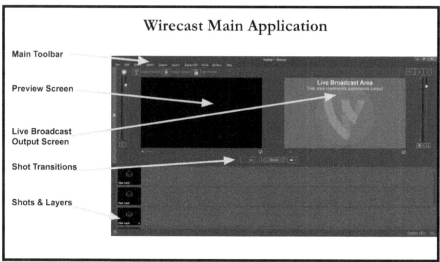

(Wirecast Interface)

Wirecast is designed to be flexible. Know upfront that there are many different possible video production workflows. When you first load the software, it may help to experiment with the screen's layout to get a feel for the possibilities. From the **Layout** menu, you can choose the layout of your main window. From the very top of the menu, you can turn on or off the **Final Mix** audio controls, shown to the left and right of the upper part of the window.

(Wirecast Layout and Audio Mixer)

Show Live and Preview, Show Preview Only, and Show Live Only allow you to toggle through the display modes showing one or two views in the upper window. Which option works best for you will depend on your production workflow. These options can also be controlled by the green and red selection buttons in the screen's upper right-hand corner.

The top half of the interface is the Broadcast area. This is where you can view the Preview and the Live Output.

Preview

When displayed, the **Preview** window shows what will go to your live broadcast when you press the transition button. Within the **Preview** window, you can manipulate an image using the handlebars to adjust its size, position, and rotation. These changes will not be reflected in the live view until you press the transition button.

Live

The **Live** window shows what is being sent to the output of your production. Whether you are recording or live streaming, this is what is being captured. The Pro version of Wirecast can also record multiple shots at once using the **ISO** recording feature.

(Muted vs Un-Muted Headphones Monitoring)

Audio Levels Mix

To the left of the **Preview** window and the right of the **Live** window are the audio meters. With these, you can monitor and adjust the audio gain. By default, the audio levels in the preview screen will not play through your headphones. When the audio levels are muted you will see a gray headphone icon with a strike through it. When the audio levels are active you will see the headphone icon in green.

(Muting and Unmuting Speakers)

Below the audio levels next to the **Final Mix** is a speaker button and a headphone button. The speaker button is used to mute the audio of the whole broadcast and the headphone button mutes the audio generally used for monitoring the broadcast. In this way, you can turn off your headphones for monitoring the broadcast and toggle between monitoring an audio source in preview. Most users only monitor the broadcast output for simplicity.

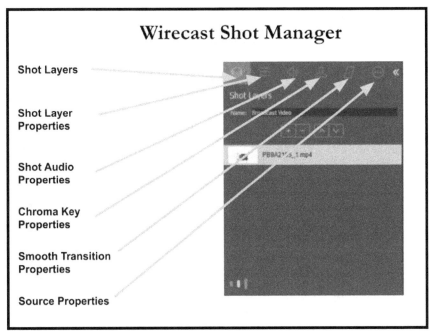

(Wirecast Shot Manager Area)

Shot Manager Box

To the left of the **Preview Window** is the **Shot Manager** box. If it is not there, click on the two arrows on the main window's far left. The **Shot Manager** is hidden by default to save space. There are tabs for shot layers within this box to edit the shot's layer properties, audio, chroma key properties, smooth transition properties, and system device properties. The content of these windows will vary depending on the shot selected in the Main Shot List.

This is the area of Wirecast where you can customize the media you are working with. For example, you can layer together multiple pieces of media together and build one awesome shot that you can transition to with a click of a button. It is here that you can chromakey out a green background and manage the layers of your production to create a virtual set or dynamic scene.

Transition Bar

Between the **Live** and **Preview** windows and the Main Shot Layers is the **Transition Bar**. The **Transition Bar is** covered in the next chapter. This area controls switching from one source to another and enables you to choose transition styles and effects.

Main Shot List

At the bottom of the interface is the Main Shot List consisting of five layers organized in rows. Each row is used to mix together media inside of the **Preview** window before it's moved to the **Live** window. You therefore have a choice as to whether you want to build custom shots with multiple layers in the Shot Manager, or use the layering system to build dynamic layouts in real time.

In general, it's best practice to put your cameras and live capture sources on the bottom layers and your top level graphics on the upper layers. This is because, as you mix shots together in preview, they will be mixed together in a layered system. This is a great way to think about creating dynamix productions that can be updated quickly. Producers can choose a bottom level camera or live video source and then quickly choose middle or top level graphics. A middle level graphics might be a lower third and a top level graphics could be a logo or a social media post.

Advanced transitions can also be managed in the "**Smooth Transitions Properties**" area of the **Shot Managers Box**.

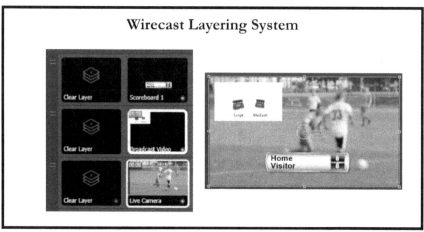

(Wirecast Layering System)

Control/Status Bar

(Wirecast Control & Status Notification Bar)

Across the top of the interface is the status bar. This shows you the current state of your **Stream**, **Recording**, and **ISO** recording. There are time counters for all three, and the icons change colors to represent the state of the recording or stream.

4 CONNECTING CAMERAS & CAPTURING SOURCES

Using Wirecast for live video production often requires the connection of a couple cameras. You can connect cameras to your computer running Wirecast in a variety of ways that you will learn about in this chapter. These options include internal capture cards, external capture devices, USB, IP streams and NDI.

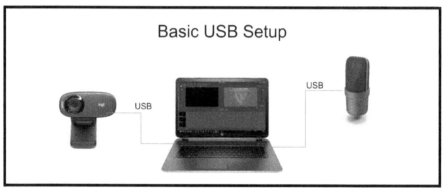

(Simple USB streaming setup with USB connected webcam and microphone)

USB Webcams

Setting up a compatible USB webcam is easy. Simply plug your webcam into your computer. Next open Wirecast, add a **new shot**, select the **Video Capture** category, and select your device from the menu. Once it is added to the **Main Shot Window**, you can click on it and make any necessary adjustments on the **System Device Properties** tab in the **Shot Manager Box**.

Capture Cards

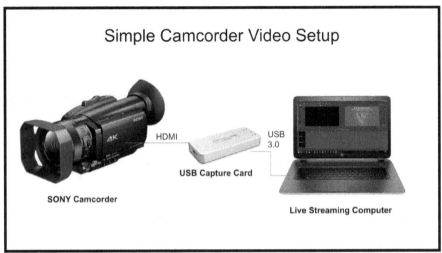

Simple Camcorder Video Setup

HDMI — USB Capture Card — USB 3.0

SONY Camcorder

Live Streaming Computer

(Simple more professional capture card setup with Wirecast and a Camcorder)

To connect a camera with an HDMI or SDI output, you will need an internal PCIe capture card or an external USB capture device. Some capture card models even have options to connect to older standards like composite (RCA) or component (YPbPr) video. Capture card devices can be installed internally in PCs computers using a PCIe card slot. If you only need to capture one or two cameras you can use available USB ports to connect USB capture cards. These USB capture cards convert an HDMI or SDI video signal into a usable USB connection with Wirecast. You can also use a Thunderbolt connection to connect additional cameras to your computer.

One of the most significant constraints to capturing cameras with a computer is the available card slots or ports on your computer. You can add additional USB ports to your computer through a USB hub but it is not recommended for use with a camera. This is because USB hubs create a bandwidth bottleneck in your capture system. When using USB connections to capture cameras, it's never a good idea to use a USB Hub. If you are running out of USB ports on your computer, use a Hub for low-bandwidth devices like your keyboard and mouse. Use your dedicated USB 3.0 or USB C connections for cameras to ensure proper bandwidth channels.

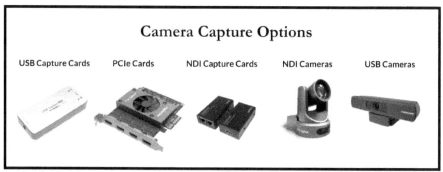

(Additional capture card options for connecting sources to Wirecast)

Pro Tip: If you are having trouble with capturing a camera try moving around the USB ports that you are using. Sometimes two or more USB ports will share the same internal chipsets. For example, if you have a laptop with two USB ports on either side, each side might share a single USB chipset. Therefore it would be better to connect one camera on each side to optimize your available USB bandwidth.

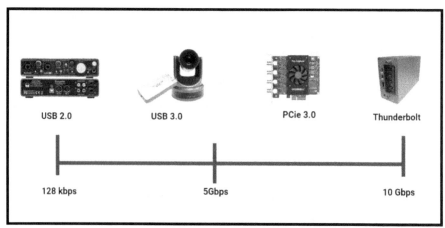

(USB Bandwidth Chart)

The above chart outlines the various bandwidth capabilities of USB 2.0, USB 3.0, PCIe and Thunderbolt connections. USB 2.0 can handle up to 480 Mbps, but in this example we are showing an audio device using only 128 kbps. USB 2.0 connections are ideal for audio mixers, keyboards, mice and controllers. USB 3.0 connections are ten times faster than USB 2.0, and they are ideal for capturing cameras. An uncompressed 1080p camera set to 30 frames per second will use roughly 1.5 Gbps of USB bandwidth. PCIe connections come in a variety of types, but they are generally faster than USB 3.0 connections. A PCIe 3.0 connection can support up to 32 Gbps which is more than enough for four 1080p60fps cameras. Finally, thunderbolt connections are a great option for many users especially if you have a Mac. Thunderbolt connections can support up to 17 Gbps by current specifications which are also great for bringing multiple cameras into your computer. The Thunderbolt connection box listed above is called the PTZOptics Producer+ upgrade box which provides 4 SDI connections to a computer using the Thunderbolt connections.

Pro Tip: Once you have installed your capture device, be sure that you download the device manufacturer's latest drivers. Setting up a capture card with your camera and computer should be fairly simple. The best place to find support for issues with capture devices is at the website of the manufacturer. There are also often helpful threads available in the Wirecast User Forum as well.

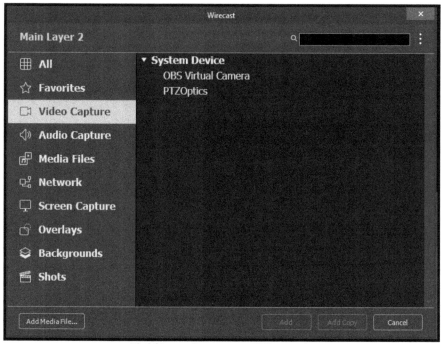

(Adding a Source to Wirecast)

Once your capture device is connected and configured, you can add it as a shot in the **Main Shot List** by choosing it from the **Video Capture** category. Once the shot has been captured you may need to make some adjustments on the **System Device Properties** tab in the **Shot Manager Box** to align the settings with your camera and capture device.

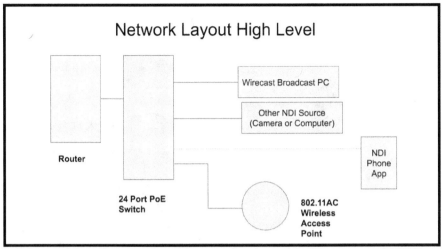

(Networking diagram for video production with Wirecast and NDI)

NDI Sources

NDI™ stands for **Network Device Interface** and it's a simple way to connect IP video sources to Wirecast and other applications over your Local Area Network. A Local Area Network or LAN, is the network that connects your computer to the router which provides your computer internet. This book will include a more detailed description on NDI and networking in an upcoming chapter. For now, simply understand that NDI is a simple way to send and receive video over the network that your computer is connected to. If there is another computer connected to the same network for example, it can receive the video from your Wirecast system and display it up on a television. Another example, might be a computer on your network that can easily send video into your Wirecast system. A popular use case for NDI is a laptop that is set up to send video to a Wirecast system that consists of PowerPoint presentation slides. In order to do this, the laptop can use the free NDI tools available from NewTek to capture and send NDI video from one computer to another.

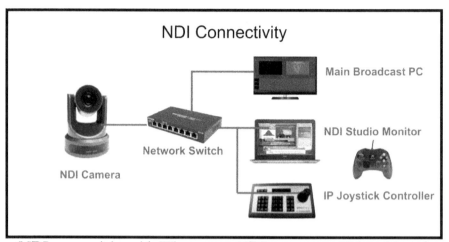

(NDI connectivity with Wirecast, an NDI camera, an IP joystick and NDI Studio Monitor)

The example above shows a PTZOptics NDI camera connected to a network switch. This network switch is also connected to a Main Broadcast PC running Wirecast, another computer running NDI Studio Monitor and an IP joystick. The Main Broadcast PC is able to bring the PTZOptics NDI camera connection into Wirecast using the **Network Source** option.

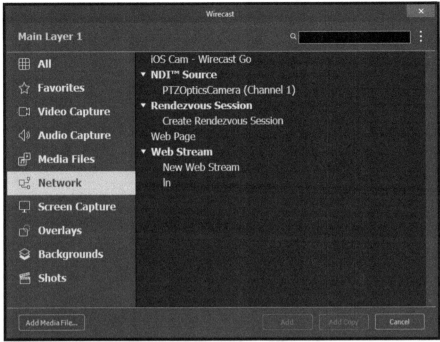

(Adding network sources to Wirecast)

NDI Sources available on your network will automatically show up under the **NDI Source** area of **Network** when you add sources to Wirecast. Additionally, there is a laptop running the free NDI Studio Monitor tool which is being used to view the output of Wirecast. This is an easy way to distribute video over your network using additional computers. NDI Studio Monitor can also be used with a USB connected XBox controller to control PTZOptics cameras. An IP Joystick connected to the network is another great way to control cameras on your network.

Pro Tip: Computers running NDI Studio Monitor can be remotely controlled using a special IP address that shows up when you launch Studio Monitor. Try using this IP address on another computer to remotely change the NDI source the computer is displaying.

5 WIRECAST SHOTS AND LAYERS

One of the unique features of Wirecast is the way it organizes media sources that are part of your production. The software uses two terms, **Shot** and **Layer**, to describe the interface on how it works.

(Plus button for adding a shot to Wirecast)

Shots

Shots are the basis of any production. A shot is made up of some type of media, be it sound or video, and any associated settings. At the most basic level, a shot can be just one piece of media such as a camera feed, video clip, or graphics. However, the real power of a shot lies when multiple elements of media are combined. Media can be combined or "layered" for more complex and visually appealing shots. This could include a camera shot with a separate sound source, overlaid title, and/or additional graphics. A shot can even be a playlist of shots rotating on a preset basis.

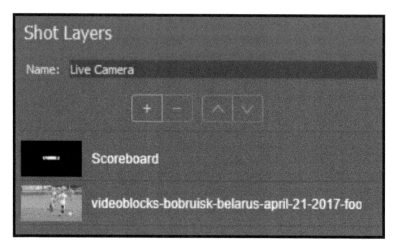

(Editing Shot and adding Layers)

Layers

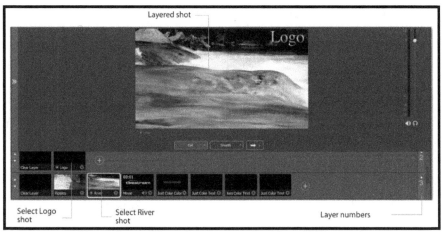

(Overview of layering system inside of Wirecast)

To create rich multimedia shots, Wirecast uses the concept of layers. When you look at the **Main Shot List** window, you will see a total of five layer rows. To assemble a shot, you can select one source from each layer just by clicking on it. You cannot choose multiple shots in the same layer, but you can select one shot from each layer. All of them will be displayed in the **Preview Window** (or the Live Window if you are using Auto Live). They are displayed in a layered manner, with layer one being on top, five on the bottom, and the rest in between. If the source in layer one is opaque and fills the whole screen, you won't see the rest of the sources in the window. However, by resizing sources and using different types of overlays and transparencies, the five layers can create a visually rich shot. Layers will be covered in more depth in another chapter.

Layer Windows

By default, the **Main Shot List** and the five included layers are positioned at the bottom of the main window. However, for more flexibility, each layer can also be displayed in its own separate window. This may be helpful, especially to users with multiple or large screens.

Any layer can be opened in a new window using the Window menu and selecting New Layer Window. Everything works the same way. You just get the option of moving your layer windows independently.

LED Indicators

Red and Green LED indicators in the **Main Shot List** can help you keep track of what sources are being used at any time. A green LED on a source indicates that it is currently selected and showing in the **Preview** window. A red LED indicates that it is presently in use for the main output and is shown in the **Live** window. If a source is in both the **Live** and **Preview** windows, it will be marked with a red LED.

6 COMMON SOURCES

Add Shot Menu

To add sources to the **Main Shot List,** just hover over any layer and click the Plus Button (+). This will open the **Add Shot** menu, which will show you all the categories of sources you can add. The first category is **Favorites**. This provides easy access to your most-used sources. You can add any source to that menu by clicking the star next to it.

(Star button is used to develop a favorite list of sources in Wirecast)

Video Capture

This is where you can add any compatible camera or capture devices directly connected to your computer. This includes USB cameras and webcams, including many models from Microsoft, Logitech, and PTZOptics. Wirecast can use capture cards from popular manufacturers like AJA, Aver Media, Blackmagic, Elgato (Windows version only), Epiphan, and Magewell. Wirecast also supports cameras connected over a network connection such as IP or NDI. These can be added in the **Network** category below.

Audio Capture

Audio sources are added in this category. You may be receiving the system sound from your computer, audio directly from a camera, or using an attached system device to capture audio from an external source. All of the possible sources, including virtual sources, will be listed and can be added here.

Media Files

Video, audio, and image files can be added here or by using the **Add Media File** button at the bottom of this menu box. When adding files using this category, you can also add media from the **Wirecast Stock Media Library**.

Network

The **Network** category opens up the possibility of capturing audio and video over your local network connection. This is where you can select IP or NDI sources such as cameras or video feeds. You can also capture displays or streams from the web. Two important Wirecast features can also be accessed here, the **iOS cam**, part of the **Wirecast Go iOS app**, and **Rendezvous** sessions, which allow you to bring remote video guests into your production.

Screen Capture

Wirecast gives you the option to capture any monitor or window on your local computer for use as a shot. You can also use the **Remote Desktop Presenter**, on any other computer on your network. On Mac computers, you can also capture the screen of any iPhone or iPad connected via a compatible lightning cable. NDI tools are also a great way to capture content from other computers on your network.

Overlays

The category includes custom sources mainly intended to be in the top layer of any shot to overlay other source content. You have the option of adding a clock, image carousel, QR code, scoreboard, text, animated titles, and lower thirds. All of these are editable and have customization options. You also have the option of adding a Twitter feed to your production as an overlay,

Backgrounds

You can further customize your production by adding custom backgrounds, including solid color, a web page, or even a virtual set. Wirecast comes with several built-in virtual set backgrounds, and more are available from third-party sellers.

7 WORKING WITH WIRECAST'S LAYERS

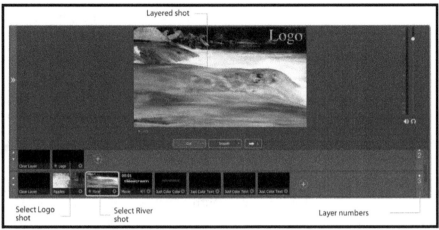

(Layering system inside of Wirecast)

If you have used other live video production software, the layers in Wirecast may seem a little different. Once you understand how they work and all of the possibilities they allow you to create, you will find them to be one of the best features of the software.

At the bottom of the Wirecast main window, the Main Shot List shows five individual layers. The layers might be best understood by thinking of a stack of five photos. Obviously, the photo on the very top, the top layer, will obscure everything underneath it. But if the picture on top was smaller, had holes in it, or was semi-transparent, you could see some of the photos behind it.

So, for instance, you might have a small clock on the top layer, leaving the rest of the screen for the next layer, maybe a sports scoreboard that also doesn't take up a lot of room. Behind that you may want to have a video shot on a green screen with the green keyed out showing the background image I have on the next layer. The bottom layer could be audio from a microphone or other source since no-one needs to see that. This enables you to easily create complex multi-media shots with just a few clicks. You can choose any source from each layer, quickly creating new audio and visual canvas from all your different elements.

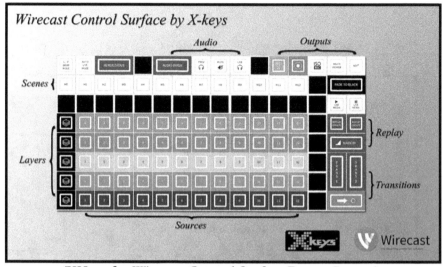

(XKeys for Wirecast Control Surface Button Layout)

The above picture shows a special control surface designed by Xkeys for controlling Wirecast. The layout is a great representation of how your can control Wirecast. As you can see, there are scenes at the very top which you can use. There are special buttons for managing video callers and audio sources. But you will notice, that the majority of the real estate is used for managing layers.

The layering system provides great versatility since you can change the shot in each layer with just a click while keeping all of the other layers the same. You can also clear the content of any layer by clicking on the **Clear Layer** tile on the left. Shots can be moved from layer to layer by dragging and dropping. The same shot can even appear in multiple layers. For instance, you can put a camera in layer one when you want it in the forefront and then again in layer three for when you want it to be shown behind overlays. You can also move entire layers up and down inside of Wirecast by dragging and dropping the layer from the left hand side.

In Wirecast, you can also create layers within a single shot. If there is a collection of layers that you want to access with one click, make a shot with your primary source and then click on the **Shot Layers** tab in the **Shot Manager Box**. Here you can add additional shots as layers and rearrange the position of the shots as needed.

Once you get the hang of layers, you will see that Wirecast gives you both the ability to preset complex shots for use in productions and also make fast changes to your shots on the fly.

8 TRANSITIONS AND AUTO-LIVE

One of the most basic functions of any live video production software is switching from one shot to another seamlessly. Switching may be from one camera to another, a camera to a pre-recorded video, or even between still images or other video sources. With Wirecast, you have two main options for transitions, AutoLive, and the Go button.

The Go Button

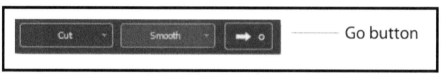

(Wirecast Transition buttons)

The **Go Button** can be found on the transition bar, located between the **Broadcast Area** and the **Main Shot List**. To the left of the **Go Button** are the transition options. In the Preferences menu, you can choose how many transition options you wish to display (0-3). While you can only use one transition at a time, displaying multiple options makes it faster and easier to switch between transition types. Whenever more than one option is shown, you can switch back and forth by just clicking and highlighting your selected transition type.

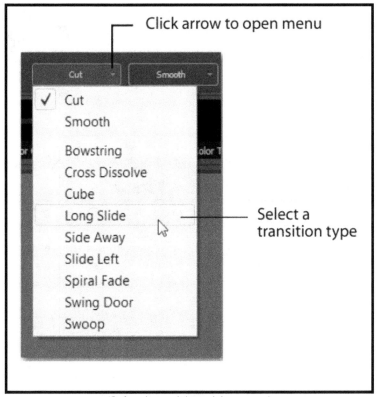

(Selecting a Transition type)

In the dropdown menus, you can choose the style of transition. When cut is selected, the transition will be executed immediately. With smooth, the transition fades in or out. You can also choose from many other more stylistic transition styles like 3D plane, bands, circle wipe, fade to black, and swap.

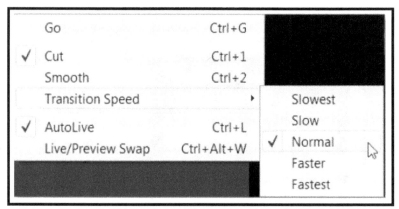

(Choosing a Transition Speed)

On the main menu at the top of the screen, under the **Switch** menu, the **Transition Speed** can be set from its slowest to fastest setting. The preferred switching type, style and speed will be executed when the Go button is pressed.

Another critical option is based on your preference for what happens to the **Preview Window** when you press the **Go Button**. By default, what is in **Preview** will stay in **Preview** after it is sent to live. This is useful if you feel that you may need to make some changes and send it to **Live** again. However, under the **Switch Menu**, you can select **Live/Preview Swap**. With this turned on, when you press the **Go Button**, whatever is in **Preview** will go the **Live**, and whatever is in **Live** will be sent back to **Preview**. You will notice this because the Go button will turn to a double arrow.

AutoLive

(Wirecast AutoLive notification LED)

The **AutoLive** function in Wirecast reduces the number of steps required to switch scenes. This can be especially helpful when Wirecast is used by a presenter who is also controlling the software. In **AutoLive** mode, there is no preview function. Selecting a shot from the shot list will automatically make that shot live. Whatever you select will immediately be sent to the output of the production. There is no need to use the **Go Button** or **Preview** window with this setting. However, when adjustments are made to the shot in the **Preview** window, they will be made in the **Live** window upon pressing the **Go Button**.

Best Practices

There are best practices when it comes to producing a show from the perspective of the technical director. A well produced show is essentially an orchestrated process of capturing the show's content with your audiovisual equipment. In order to do this, the technical director (Wirecast User) has to make decisions about how and when to transition between the available video and audio sources. The goal of a good technical director is to produce a cohesive storyline. As you transition between one scene to the next, it's important to think about the viewer's experience as they follow along with your production's storyline. Choosing the appropriate transition moments and using the correct transition type, can be essential in capturing your audience's attention and making the technology flow seamlessly.

Producers can use transition effects to complement their production capabilities. A good transition transparently leads the audience through one scene to the next. The best transition is one that keeps the audience captivated by the content. In a perfect world, the transition happens as if the viewer naturally selected it. In order to do this, your production should flow in a way that feels natural to viewers. Be careful not to use fancy transitions that could take away from the main message of your content. Let's review the four most popular transitions used in video production. In order of popularity, these would be the cut, the fade, the fade to black and the stinger transition effects.

Type	Most Commonly Used
Cut	90% of the time
Fade (Smooth)	<5%
Other	<5%

You will notice that there are quite a few options in Wirecast when it comes to video transition effects. The most commonly used video transition is a cut. The cut simply switches two video sources in a direct cut transition without any noticeable special effects. The cut should be used for transitioning between most of your prepared content. The cut is perfect for transitioning between two live camera angles in the same scene. When you are cutting between multiple camera angles that you have in one scene, it is important to think about the camera angles. Jumping to too many different camera angles, too quickly could be disorienting for your viewers.

A good technical director will visualize the camera angles that they have available and move through them in a natural order. You should try to arrange your camera angles so that you can reveal additional details as they become more important to the story. If you have a pan, tilt and zoom camera that can capture multiple angles during a single production, consider switching back and forth between close up angles and your available wide-angle shots. Generally, you don't want to cut to a camera angle that is more than 45 degrees away from your current camera angle. In this way, you can switch between multiple cameras in an arch to finally reach a camera that may show a side or behind the scenes camera angle.

Interview diagram #1

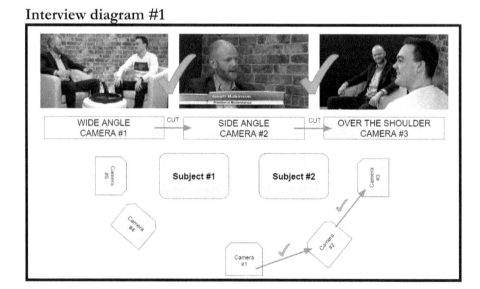

(Diagram showing production angle suggestions)

To study these production techniques let's use the example of a two-person interview. When you are producing an interview like this, it's a good idea to start with a wide angle shot that displays both of your subjects in the same shot. This is your central shot that establishes placement for the viewers in the scene that they are watching. The cut transition can then be used to enhance the viewer's perspective of each person as they take turns talking. A transition like a fade or a stinger would look unnatural for this type of production. The cut makes the camera switching feel natural and unnoticeable because it happens in the blink of an eye. Each transition should be timed to flow with the conversation your subjects are having.

Interview diagram #2

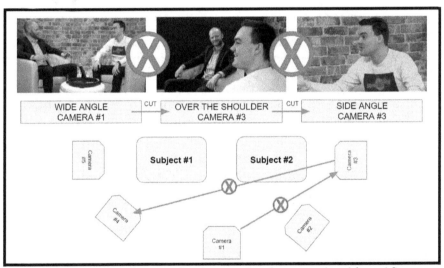

(Diagram showing production angles that you should avoid)
As you can see in the production workflow of the interview diagram #1, the producer has selected to move between the camera cuts that are sequential around the arc of camera options moving counter clockwise. Interview diagram #2 shows a sequence of transitions that do not follow sequential movements around the camera inputs that are available and beyond the 45-degree rule from the last camera angle. Using these types of "jumpy cuts" could be disorienting for viewers. Remember that all rules are meant to be broken, and every camera

setup is different. Use your instincts and create a production that makes sense for the story you want to tell. Just remember that the transition decision you make for your school announcements show will be more reserved than other video projects you may work on at home.

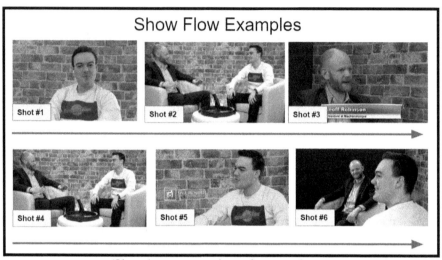

(Showing a natural production flow)

The crossfade or "Smooth" transition is perhaps the second most popular transition in live video production. You will notice that they are used much less frequently than the cut, but they are often given prime real estate in many production systems. Crossfade transitions can produce beautiful artistic visual effects. The crossfade should be used in this way to enhance your production. Crossfades are used frequently during musical performances such as the national anthem performed just before a sports event. You will notice the crossfade is used when the cameras switch between a close up of a singer and a wide panning shot of a crowd. You will notice great crossfade transitions that feature the American flag slowly fading into a crowd of singing sports fans.

If you have an artistic shot prepared for your next video production project, the crossfade may be the most appropriate transition to use. If you have a pan, tilt and zoom camera, try transitioning with the crossfade when the camera is in between a slow pan. Many professional broadcast studios use a physical T-bar to create custom cross-fade transitions between multiple video inputs. Use this transition sparingly and note that crossfades may look pixelated in low bitrate bandwidth streams.

The fade to black sometimes shortened to just "FTB", is perhaps the next most commonly used video transition. You can fade to black and fade from black to notify the beginning or the end of your production. This type of video transition clearly demonstrates the nonverbal communication power you have as a producer. Try using the fade to black transition to close a unique scene or segment of your morning announcements show. If you can time your fade to black with the ending points of an audio track, you will really be doing great. Hopefully, your audio director will work in sync and fade the audio track for you as the video fades to black.

9 CAPTURING MONITORS, WINDOWS AND APPLICATIONS

Wirecast offers you the option to capture high-quality video content from your local computer and incorporate it into your video. These screen captures can come from a monitor, window, or active software application. This same functionality is also available from another computer on your local network using the **Remote Desktop Presenter**.

Capturing a Local Source

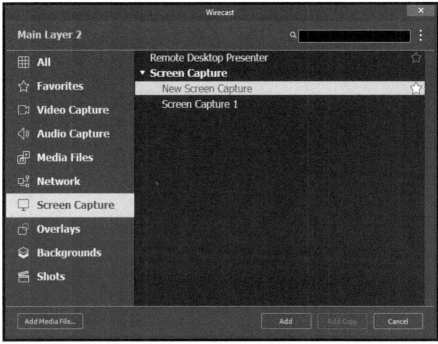

(Screen capture options in Wirecast)

To add a screen capture source, click the Plus (**+**) button in one of the layers as though you were adding any other type of shot. Choose the **Screen Capture** category on the left and then **New Screen Capture** on the right. In the **Screen Capture Properties** dialogue box to the left, you can name your source. Next, from the dropdown menu, choose the type of source you wish to capture: a specific monitor, a window from an application, or a game. The game option allows you to capture video from a particular game at a higher framerate of 60fps as compared to a standard 30fps.

Next, you have the option of showing or hiding your cursor using the check box and whether or not you want to capture audio as well. You can then configure the captured shot. If you are capturing a monitor, you will see a dialogue box listing available monitors. You will also have the option to capture the entire monitor or select a specific region. If you choose to share an application, the dialogue box will show you all active applications in a dropdown box. If your application is not listed, be sure it is currently running and hit the refresh button. If your chosen application has multiple windows open, you can select the appropriate window from the dropdown menu.

Keep in mind that while you can only select one screen capture source per shot, you can create as many shots as you want. This makes it easy to switch back and forth between monitors or applications or even show multiple screens captured side by side or tiled in one window.

Using Remote Desktop Presenter

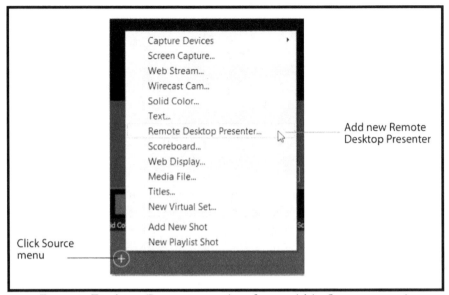

(Remote Desktop Presenter option from within Source menu)

There are many situations where you may want to capture content from another computer and feed it into your production. **Wirecast Remote Desktop Presenter** makes this easy. As long as the other computer is connected to your Local Area Network (LAN), you can easily incorporate content from a monitor, window, or application and create a shot that can be used just like any other media source.

The first step to using Remote Desktop Presenter is installing it on the computer (Mac or PC) you wish to capture. Anyone can download the free software at www.telestream.net/dtp. Once the software is installed and running, it can be configured. The configuration only offers a couple of options. You can share a monitor or screen region on a monitor or any window of a specific application. At this point, you can also decide if you wish to send system audio along with the video. The Desktop Presenter will begin sending video immediately. However, you will notice that there is a pause button in the bottom right of the settings menu if, at any point, you wish to stop sending video and audio. The resume button will restart the feed. Before you leave the remote computer, be sure to write down or otherwise capture the TCP/IP address. This will enable you to connect to this remote computer back in Wirecast.

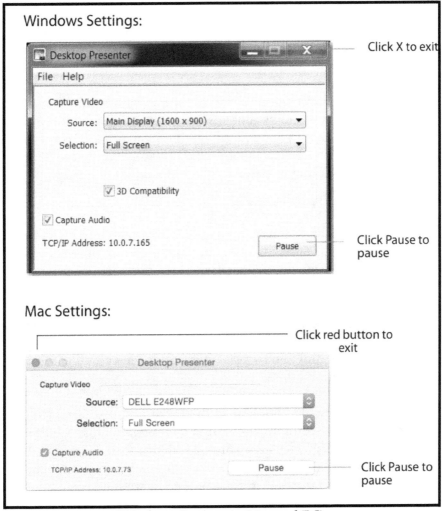

(Windows Settings in Mac and PC)

Now, you can add this Remote Desktop Presenter source in Wirecast just like any other source. Click the Plus (+) button in one of the layers, choose Screen Capture from the left and New Remote Desktop Presenter from the right. Now in the settings box to the left, name the source, enter the IP address from the other computer, and select whether you want to receive audio. Once you apply those settings, you should see your remote source in the preview window.

10 EDITING SHOTS

Once you have added a shot in Wirecast, you have many tools at your disposal to manipulate its contents and create the production you want. Images and videos can be resized, repositioned, rotated, and scaled with intuitive controls. Editing shots occur in both the **Preview Window** and the **Shot Manager Box**.

Shot Layers

In addition to the five master layers in Wirecast, each shot can have up to 50 sublayers. For many, it may be easier to setup sublayers before a live production and simple switch to a shot that has been set up perfectly during a live stream. Layers built in the **Preview Window** will work the same way in that they do in the **Shot Layers** tab of the **Shot Manager Box**. You can add and rearrange layers within the shot and then manipulate any of those layers using the controls in the **Preview Window**. The same can be done in the **Shot Layer Tab** in the **Shot Manager Box**.

You can click on any shot in the **Main Shot List** to select it to see its properties in the **Shot Manager Box**. If you wish to use the **Preview** window controls, you will need to be sure that there is no layer on top of it blocking it from view. Once the shot is selected, if it contains multiple sub-layers, select it in the properties window, to edit the layer you wish to manipulate. Keep in mind that, even if this shot is currently in your live window, changes made here will not go live until you hit the **Go Button** to transition to live.

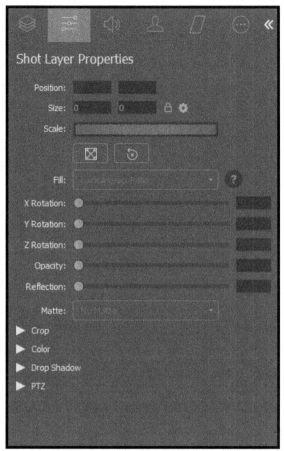

(Shot adjustment area)

The **Shot Layer Properties** window shows all of the manipulation controls. Controls include position, size, scale, x rotation, y rotation, z rotation, and opacity. By expanding the subheadings below, you can access even more control options. You can crop and adjust color properties, including brightness, contrast, gamma, hue, and saturation. Some image effects available on this menu included the ability to add either a reflection or drop shadow to the image in any layer.

Many of the same controls are also available in the **Preview** window. When a layer is selected, controls become visible surrounding the image. The image can be clicked and dragged anywhere within the window. Scaling is done by clicking any of the handlebars on the edges and corners and pulling in or out. For non-proportional scaling, just click and hold the shift key. Rotation on the Z-axis can be done using the handlebar in the center of the image. It can be pulled and extended outward for more refined control. X and Y rotation can only be done in the Shot Layer Properties window, but you can see the changes take effect immediately in the Preview window. To crop an image in the preview window, click and drag on the layer's edges while holding the control key on PC or the command key on Mac.

11 USING NDI SOURCES

NDI, or **Network Device Interface**, is a protocol developed by NewTek that makes it easier than ever to share video over IP networks. As manufacturers and developers continue to create new NDI compatible hardware and software, producers gain more options to add video sources without running traditional HDMI or SDI cabling. As long as an NDI device or computer can be added to the local area network, it can be shared with other NDI software and equipment.

Some popular NDI sources include cameras, capture devices, switchers, graphics and screen captures.

Wirecast makes it easy to set up and use NDI sources in your productions. Adding an NDI camera, capture device, or other source is mostly the same as adding any other media source type. For best results, be sure that your NDI source is on and active before launching Wirecast. Also, be sure that your Wirecast computer and your source are on the same local area network.

Click the Plus (**+**) button in the main shot list and select the **Network** category on the left. Your NDI source should appear on the list on the right. Select the source, and then in the **Source Properties** box to the left, you can see your settings. In that box, you can adjust the bandwidth of the source. This is helpful if you are having latency issues with the source. Lowering the bandwidth will reduce the source's quality, but it will also improve transmission speed and delay when that is an issue.

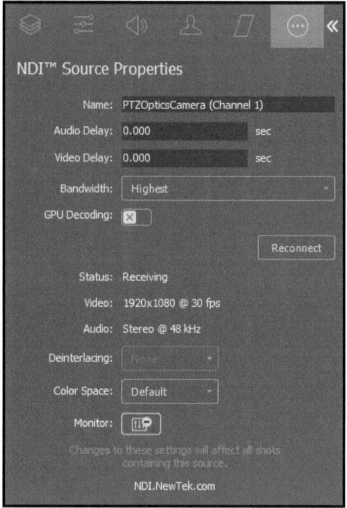

(NDI source properties in Wirecast)

Troubleshooting

If you have any trouble connecting NDI sources, there are some simple solutions to some common issues. If your NDI source does not appear in the list of sources in Wirecast, the best first step is to close and restart Wirecast. If your source still does not appear, the next recommended step is to download and install an NDI monitoring application from NewTek or Sierra. Running one of those programs will allow you to see if your computer is receiving the signal from your

NDI source. If your source is visible in the NDI monitor but is still not showing up in Wirecast, it is recommended that you reboot your computer.

If you still don't see your source, there are a few other things to try.

1. Check to be sure your Wirecast Computer and NDI source are on the same network and subdomain.
2. See if your device's firmware is up to date.
3. Determine if a firewall may be blocking network traffic.
4. Is the network configured to not allow mDNS (the protocol behind NDI)
5. Does your network have enough bandwidth?

If you still cannot get your NDI source to work, it may be worth visiting the Telestream website or an email to Wirecast support. In an upcoming chapter, you will be invited to learn more about IP networking. IP video production is incredibly powerful and will take some networking knowledge in order to take full advantage of the benefits.

12 CONTROLLING PTZ CAMERAS

With the Pro version of Wirecast, you can remotely control PTZ (pan, tilt, zoom) cameras directly from Wirecast using the **PTZ Controller** window. This works with various PTZ cameras, including the latest models from PTZOptics. The controller works both the VISCA over IP protocol as well as the new NDI PTZ controls.

(PTZ camera controller in Wirecast)

Setting Up PTZ Camera Control

Set up your camera per manufacturer instructions, ensuring that it is connected to the same network as your Wirecast computer. You will want to obtain the camera's current IP address in order to connect it to

Wirecast. Go to the **Window** menu at the top of the screen and click
PTZ Controller to display the controller interface.

In the interface, select the PTZ camera you wish to control and then
enter the IP address. For PTZOptics cameras using VISCA over IP,
the port and VISCA address will be set automatically. Once you have
entered the IP address, click the **Connect** button to the right of the
status indicator, and it will display connected when ready.

Controlling the Camera

Once the camera is ready, you can test it by clicking anywhere in the
controller area, and the camera should respond. The **Home** button will
quickly move the camera back to its home position. There are multiple
PTZ controller options within Wirecast. These include the **Map View**,
which offers a 360-degree field of the camera's visual area. The **D-Pad**
view gives you simple up, down, left, and right buttons. And an Analog
Pad view, the camera motion is controlled through a click and drag
interface. In this view, you can also use your keyboard arrow keys.
However, you can use multiple keys at once to move the camera
simultaneously on the x and y-axis.

With all of these controller options, you also have separate controls for
the zoom, focus, exposure, and white balance. Focus, exposure, and
white balance all have both manual and automatic setting options.

Setting Presets

Once you have your camera position, zoom, focus, and other settings
where you want them, you can assign these settings a preset at the
bottom of the PTZ Controller window. Just enter the number you wish
to use and click save. You can test your preset using the **Home** button
to return the camera to its default position and then entering the preset
number and pressing **Recall**.

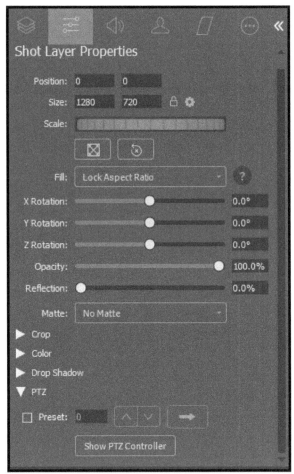

(Adding PTZ presets in Wirecast)

Setting Up A Preset as a Shot in Wirecast

PTZ camera presets can allow you to add one camera multiple times in the main shot list, each time with different settings. This means that you can have multiple virtual cameras, all with different positions and settings. With only one camera, you can have multiple positions, zoom levels, and other settings all available at any time in your main shot list.

Simply add your PTZ camera to the **Main Shot List** by clicking the Plus (**+**) button on any layer. Once added, go to the **Shot Layers Property** tab in the left corner of the main window. Go to the bottom of the menu and expand the **PTZ** options. Click to enable PTZ preset recall. Now, select the preset number you want.

You can now add this camera again to the Main Shot list and select a different preset number in the PTZ. This way when you call this shot, it will tell the PTZ camera to move to these specific PTZ preset position you have saved.

13 USING WIRECAST GO

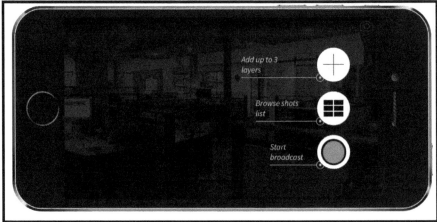

(Wirecast Go mobile App)

Another useful feature of Wirecast is the ability to use any iOS device connected to your local network as a WiFi camera using the free mobile app, Wirecast Go. Note that Wirecast Go does offer in-app purchases for additional functions and features like streaming using a mobile data network. However, all you need is the free version to capture video on your local network.

The latest version of Wirecast Go has some additional useful features like sending more than just video from the camera. With the layers function, you can easily add photos or other media from your camera to the shot you send to Wirecast.

To get started, just download the Wirecast Go app to your compatible iOS device and be sure the device is connected to the same network as your Wirecast computer. With the latest version of Wirecast and Wirecast Go, no further setup is needed. Just go to your **Main Shot List**, click the Plus (**+**) button to add a new shot. Then, select **Network** from the categories list. Your device should show up in the list under iOS Cam, Wirecast Go. If so, just click to select it. If not, select New iOS Cam - Wirecast Go. Once you have added it, just go to the **Wirecast Go Properties** menu in the upper left of the main window.

You can enter the IP address of your iOS Cam, which can be found in the settings menu of Wirecast Go.

Once you have set up your camera, you can use it like any other shot in the **Main Shot List**. Within the Wirecast Go app, you have several settings and functions to get the most out of your remote camera. In the far upper right corner, you can switch from your rear to front-facing camera. With the Plus (**+**) button, you can add two layers in addition to your camera. These can be added in front of or behind your main image. After selecting the layer you wish to adjust (front, middle, back), you can open your **Photo Gallery** to choose an image or graphic. You can change each layer's size and position, allowing you to overlay windows or create a picture in picture effect.

Under the main controls, you will also find the button to start and stop sending video, and mute or unmute audio. The gear icon opens the settings menu, which provides options for adjusting the bitrate and enabling or disabling the connection to Wirecast.

Pro Tip: Are you an Android User? Don't worry. You can purchase the NDI Camera App for Androids to send video from your phone directly into Wirecast.

14 LIVE STREAMING WITH WIRECAST

For many users, the primary function of Wirecast is to produce video content for live streaming. Everything you need to stream to one or more streaming platforms is built into Wirecast. While different streaming services require slightly different settings, the overall process for streaming remains the same.

Before Wirecast can begin streaming, you must configure your **Output Settings**. To start the configuration process, click on the **Output** menu at the top of the screen and select **Output Settings**. From the dropdown menu, select your destination.

(Live streaming Output Settings in Wirecast)

Wirecast is continually adding new content delivery network (CDN) partners but currently supports BoxCast, Churchstreaming.tv, DaCast Streaming Services, ESE Networks, High School Zoom, Jet-Stream, Lightcast, Livestream, Meridix Live Sports Platform, Onstream media, Pitchtime, SermonAudio, StreamingChurch.tv, StreamShark.io, StreamSpot, Streaming Media Hosting, Stretch Internet, Sunday Streams, Tulix Streaming, Ustream, WorshipStream, Azure Media

Services, Sermon.net, Verizon Digital Media Services, West Studio, Brightcove, Limelight, Akamai, LinkedIn Live, LiveArena, Twitter, Twitch, Vimeo, Wowza, Zixi, Facebook Live, Microsoft Stream, and YouTube are available.

If you don't see your streaming platform, click on the More button, and you can add additional options to the dropdown menu. If your destination is still not there, you will want to select **RTMP Server**, where you can set up the destination manually.

When you select your destination and click **OK**, you will see a dialogue box customized for your streaming platform. Required settings will include authentication information for your provider, encoding settings, and any other information required by your destination. Once you have confirmed all the settings, press **OK**.

Streaming to Multiple Destinations

With Wirecast, you can stream to as many destinations as your hardware and internet connection will allow. Simply add additional destinations under **Output Settings** using the "**Add…**" button. Within the dialogue box, you can click the checkbox next to each destination to toggle them on and off as needed.

(Stream notification button in Wirecast)

Once you have set up your destination(s), you can begin broadcasting by clicking on the **Stream** icon at the top of the screen. The Stream icon will blink until the connection is made. Once you are connected, the icon will turn green. The number of green bars shown at the top of the icon demonstrates the stream's connectivity and reliability level.

If there are connection issues and data packets are not reaching the server, Wirecast will buffer data packets, and the icon will turn yellow. If the problem increases and Wirecast needs to drop data packets, the icon will turn red. If the stream fails, the red failure icon will appear.

Several issues can lead to packet loss or complete failure. They can be related to your destination's servers, your internet connection, or your computer's processing power. The most common reason for problems is a lack of CPU power on the local computer. If, while streaming, you see the System CPU percentage going over 80%, you are likely to have streaming issues. You can often fix this by making adjustments to output and encoding settings and lowering the stream's quality. It is recommended that you review Wirecast's recommended system requirement to ensure your computer can handle the type of stream you wish to broadcast.

Bandwidth Considerations

Available internet bandwidth can make or break your next live event. There are multiple ways you can deliver a live or live to tape event to viewers online. When you are live streaming, it's important to understand your available bandwidth, the bitrate you should use and the resolution your project is set up to use.

Bandwidth is measured in bits per second. The word "bandwidth" is generally used to describe the data transfer rate of your internet connection available to your computer. When you measure this speed, megabits are generally used. One megabit = 1,000 kilobits. Your internet speed is measured in two ways: upload and download speed.

Resolution	Pixel Count	Frame Rate	Quality	Bitrate
4K 30fps	3840x2160	30fps	High	30Mbps
4K 30fps	3840x2160	30fps	Medium	20Mbps
4K 30fps	3840x2160	30fps	Low	10Mbps
1080p60fps	1920x1080	60fps	High	12Mbps
1080p60fps	1920x1080	60fps	Medium	9Mbps
1080p60fps	1920x1080	60fps	Low	6Mbps
1080p30fps	1920x1080	30fps	High	6Mbps

1080p30fps	1920x1080	30fps	Medium	4.5Mbps
1080p30fps	1920x1080	30fps	Low	3Mbps
720p30fps	1280x720	30fps	High	3.5Mbps
720p30fps	1280x720	30fps	Medium	2.5Mbps
720p30fps	1280x720	30fps	Low	1.5Mbps

(Recommended bitrates based on resolution, frame rate and quality of broadcast)

Think about your live stream resolution as the size of your canvas. The bitrate that you select is the amount of data that is used to fill that canvas. Therefore, you can have a high-quality 1080p stream with a bit rate of 6 Mbps, or you can have a low-quality 1080p stream with a bit rate of just 2 Mbps. Years ago, back in the time of SD (320x240 pixels), you could use flash to encode and stream at roughly 500 Kbps (That's half a Megabit). Today, most people will expect at a minimum of 720p video and a bit rate of at least 1.5 Mbps. New reports from Akamai show that most people watching 1080p video find that 6Mbps looks like excellent quality.

The chart above displays various bandwidth choices you will have for your live streams. Using this chart and your available uploads speeds, you should be able to map out the number and quality of live streams your internet connection can support. A general rule of thumb says that you should only use half of your available upload speeds for live streaming (Download speeds don't help us with live streaming). Therefore, if you have 10 Mbps of available upload speed, you should only be live streaming with 5 Mbps. Leaving headroom in your upload speeds protects your quality of service from fluctuations in the internet connection which can cause interference with your stream's consistency. Keep in mind that most live streaming software will now allow you to live stream to multiple locations at the same time.

So, you may have a choice between live streaming a single high-quality video stream, or multiple live streams of lesser quality. For example, if you have 10 Mbps of upload speed, you may create a 3 Mbps stream to YouTube and a 2Mbps stream to Facebook. If you are concerned about creating a single high-quality stream then you would only stream to YouTube using 5Mbps. Keep in mind that you can always record an incredibly high-quality recording to your local hard drive. Many production experts will record in "high bitrate" MP4 files ranging from 12-100 Mbps. The recordings saved to your local hard drive will always be of higher quality than the live streamed recordings available on YouTube and Facebook. The higher the bitrate you use, the larger your file sized will become. I generally used between 8-16 Mbps for my standard video recordings.

If you are starting to learn about bandwidth and video storage, it's important to remember Megabytes are used for files saved to a hard drive and megabits are used for streaming data on the internet. In my opinion, streaming in SD is no longer acceptable, and we have to understand the bandwidth needed to stream in HD. The minimum you want to live stream an event would be 1280x720p with a 1.5 Mbps bit rate. 720p resolutions are technically considering "High Definition" but remember that the bit rate is the accurate measure of quality when we are talking about video. So, before we talk about adaptive bitrate streaming and bandwidth calculations let's answer an important question. Should you be streaming in 720p or 1080p?

Both 720p and 1080p video resolutions are considered "High Definition". 720p is "High Definition," and 1080p is "Full High Definition." The quality of 1080p is generally better than 720p, but only if your bitrate is higher. Viewers will also need a 1080p display to watch the content. Most new mobile devices are capable of viewing content in at least 1080p quality. This is why I like to live stream in 1080p. It gives my audience a choice to view the stream quality in 1080p or scale down to lower qualities. I also like 1080p for cataloging and archiving our videos in a quality that takes full advantage of "full high definition" displays. At the end of the day, the higher the bitrate you use, the better the quality will look. So, a 720p 3Mbps video will look better than a 1080p 2Mbps video.

To answer this question for yourself, figure out exactly what your internet speeds are. Talk to your information technology department on campus about your clubs' access to bandwidth. When you speak with them, remember you are looking at your upload speeds in particular. Once you know the upload speeds you have access to, try out multiple bitrates and see which ones you think look best. There may be compromises that you have to make. Maybe you can only live stream your services to a single destination? Maybe you can only support a 720p stream because you have an older computer?

Adaptive Bit Rates

Today most CDNs are providing something called "adaptive bitrate streaming." This technology takes the best quality stream you send and breaks it down into smaller resolutions and bitrates for viewers with lower internet speeds to view in a reliable stream. CDNs such as YouTube and Facebook will use Adaptive Bitrate Streaming to optimize the video quality your viewers receive based on their available internet access. This further supports the need to stream in the highest quality possible to allow the CDN (Content Delivery Network) to make the best choices for viewers on their platform. Some CDN's also call this process "Live Cloud Encoding".

15 RECORDING VIDEO WITH WIRECAST

If you wish to record your production for local use or just want an archive backup, Wirecast makes recording to disk simple. You can record in MOV, MP4, or on a PC, as a Windows Media File (WMV). To start recording, just click on the **Record** button at the top of the main window. This will launch a dialogue box where you can choose your preferred recording format.

(Recording notification button in Wirecast)

In the next dialogue box, you can name your file. Next, you will want to pay special attention to the encoding options for your recording. Keep in mind that if you will be streaming, these can be different from your streaming encoder settings. Your settings will be primarily determined by the purpose of your recording. If you are recording just as a backup and choose smaller MP4 files, you will likely want to select an H.264 option in the resolution, frame rate, and bit rate that fits your needs. If you require a higher quality recording (for instance, if you will be importing the video into video editing software), a MOV is recommended. For that, you will want to either use an appropriate MJPEG file on PC or ProRes on Mac.

(Recording options in Wirecast)

Finally, choose the destination on your computer where you wish the file to be written and stored. Click OK, and the dialogue box will be dismissed. You can always access these settings or choose different recording options by choosing Output Settings from the Output menu.

Now when you press the Record button, your recording will begin. As long as the button remains green, your recording is active. Even if your stream stops due to a connection issue, your recording will continue.

Auto Save

In the event of a recording error, Wirecast's Auto Save function may enable you to recover your recording. All file formats, WMV, MOV, and MP4, are recoverable in 20-second increments.

Pro Tip: It's generally a good idea to record a high quality version of your production directly to your computer's hard drive. This is because you do not need to compress the video as much when it's not being live streamed. Use the **Encoding** option to choose your recordings quality. The higher the bitrate the higher the quality, just like live streams.

16 USING CHROMA, LUMA, AND COLOR KEYS

The latest version of Wirecast has improved capabilities in Chroma, Luma, and Color Keys. These features allow for background replacement and the removal of parts of an image based on color or luminosity. Properties for these features can be found in the **Chroma Key Properties** tab of the **Shot Manager Box**.

To use chroma, luma, or color keys, begin by selecting the shot you wish to use from the **Main Shot List**. For chromakey, this may be a live video shot against a green or blue screen. For luma and color keys, it may be a graphic or other image files. Click on the shot and then select the **Chroma Key Properties** tab from in the **Shot Manager Box**. At the top of the box, you will see a dropdown menu that will allow you to select between chroma, luma, and color keys. The **Use** checkbox next to the dropdown menu toggles the effect on and off.

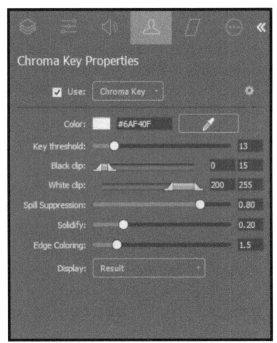

(Chroma key options in Wirecast)

Chroma Keys

Using a chroma key is the process of selecting one specific color in a video, removing it, and replacing it (keying it) with a different background. This effect is most commonly known from television weather reporters who stand in front of a green screen which is replaced, on our screens, by the weather map.

When you click the Use checkbox, Wirecast will apply the effect, and you can fine-tune the setting with tools down below. The color will be set based on the image. However, you can fine-tune the color to be removed using the color's hex number or using the dropper tool.

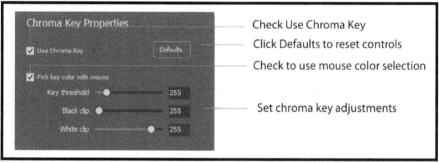

(Using the Chroma Key options inside of Wirecast)

Using the sliders, you can also adjust the key threshold, representing how far away from the chroma color you want to be replaced. The Black Clip allows you to make adjustments to how the effect interprets black. If you notice black areas keyed out, you will need to adjust this. This is the same for the White Clip slider. If you see white areas of your shot keyed out, you can make adjustments here.

The Spill Suppression slider is a useful tool for removing any green or blue reflections that may come from your background. This is usually found on the edges of the subject in the shot. In making adjustments in settings like this, you may want to go to the Shot Layer Properties tab and increase the scale so that you can more clearly see the edges.

The Solidify slider adjusts the degree to which the effect interprets pixels around the key as being part of the key. This can help to smooth out rough edges between the subject and the key. Finally, Edge

Coloring can help eliminate the halo effect often seen on keyed images by pulling colors from inside the keyed object's boundaries. Working with Spill Suppression, Solidify, and Edge Coloring can help you perfect the look of your object against the background.

Luma Keys

Luma Keys work in a similar way except, in this case, the key is determined based on intensity while ignoring color values. This is often used with logos or other graphics with a white or black background that needs to be removed so that the new background image can show through. With Luma Keys, the options are simplified with only sliders for Black Clip, White Clip, and Edge Coloring.

Color Keys

Color keys are also useful for logos and graphics. Instead of basing the key on intensity, in this case, it is based on color. This can easily remove any non-white background or other elements of an image. For color keys, the Chroma Key Properties window gives you options to set the color to be replaced and adjust the Alpha Clip and Edge Coloring sliders to fine-tune the color removal.

17 USING WIRECAST WITH ZOOM

Zoom has become an industry standard for bringing people together for online video conferencing. Zoom is a powerful tool, but there are situations where you need more power and flexibility for the video you share. Using Wirecast with Zoom gives you access to all of Wirecast's features, including layers, graphics, virtual backgrounds, screen sharing, and transitions. To connect Wirecast to Zoom, you will need to use the **Virtual Camera** function.

Using Wirecast in a Zoom Meeting

In Wirecast, go to **Virtual Camera Out** under the **Output** dropdown menu. Be sure that Flip Video Horizontally is checked. If you would also like the audio from Wirecast to be a part of your Zoom meeting, be sure that Virtual Microphone is also checked. Then click Start. You may see a dialog box prompting you to install the Wirecast Virtual Camera. If so, simply follow the prompts.

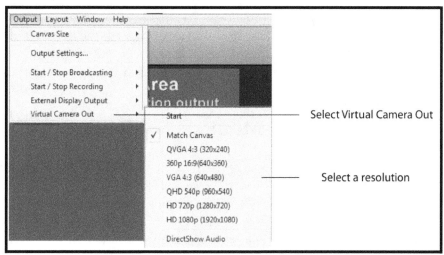

(Virtual camera output options in Wirecast)

Now open Zoom and start your meeting if you have not already started it. Find the camera icon at the bottom of the screen, click on the up arrow next to it and select Wirecast Virtual Camera. You can also click on **Video** settings if you wish to make any adjustments.

(Connecting a Virtual Camera from Wirecast to Zoom)

To use Wirecast audio, click on the up arrow next to the microphone icon at the bottom left of the screen and select Wirecast Virtual Microphone. You can also click **Audio** settings if you wish to test or adjust the audio settings.

Bringing a Zoom Meeting into Wirecast

It is also possible that you want to include a remote Zoom participant into Wirecast. To do this, you will take advantage of Wirecast's Screen Capture Option. Make sure Zoom is running, and your meeting is started. Next, add a new shot to the **Main Shot List**. Choose the **Screen Capture** category on the left and choose new screen capture.

In the **Shot Manager Box**, choose the **Screen Capture Properties** tab. In the dropdown menu next to **Capture Type**, select window. Then, next to select **Window/Monitor**, click **Configure**. For application, choose Zoom.us and for Window, choose Zoom meeting.

To capture the audio on a Windows PC, be sure that the **Capture System Audio** checkbox is checked.

On Mac computers, the process of capturing audio from Zoom is more complicated. While it is simple to send virtual audio to Zoom, the return audio currently requires third-party software. Options like Black Hole and VB-Cable will allow you to send audio from Zoom and capture it as an audio capture source in Wirecast. Once your third-party software is installed and ready, simply choose the software's virtual destination as a speaker output in Zoom and then add it as a shot using the Audio Capture category and selecting the system device.

18 USING AN ELGATO STREAMDECK

You can significantly improve your Wirecast workflow by adding a physical controller such as the Elgato Stream Deck, Stream Deck Mini, or Stream Deck XL. This is easy to set up thanks to the Elgato Stream Deck Wirecast plugin. Once set up, the Stream Deck can mimic the Wirecast interface and give you physical buttons to select shots, clear layers, transition, and access other Wirecast features. The Stream Deck integration is a great way to improve your workflow and add tactile control.

(Elgato StreamDeck)

Installing the Stream Deck Software

To easily integrate your Stream Deck, go to elgato.com, click on downloads, and download the current version of the software for your Elgato product and computer. Follow all of the prompts to complete the install. Next, install the Wirecast plugin. Go to the bottom right corner of the program and click on the More Actions box. Next, go to the search box in the menu bar and enter Wirecast. Once the search is complete, click Install next to the Wirecast listing.

Connecting and Setting up Your Stream Deck

Before going any further, plug your Stream Deck into your computer's USB port. If it is properly connected, the light will come on. To see how to add shots to the Stream Deck interface, it is helpful to set up some shots in Wirecast, so open Wirecast and ensure that you have at least two shots on two different layers in the Main Shot List.

Now return the Stream Deck application. Under the Wirecast tab, you can click and drag the Clear Layer for each layer and any shots you created in Wirecast. You can arrange these any way you want, but you may find it helpful to mimic the Wirecast software interface. Once you have dragged and organized your shots, you can add any additional commands you want to the Stream Deck by dragging and dropping. These may include the Stream button, the Record button, the Go button, and the AutoLive button.

When you return to Wirecast, you can see the Stream Deck buttons now replicating the software interface controls.

19 USING WIRECAST RENDEZVOUS

Wirecast makes it simple to add remote guests to your live video production using the built-in peer-to-peer conferencing and screen sharing platform, Rendezvous. Guests can be added from anywhere in the world as long as they have a computer or smart device with a strong wired, WiFi, or LTE connection, with enough bandwidth to send video and audio.

Sufficient bandwidth is critical, and you will want to test both your guests' connections and the bandwidth of your local connection to ensure that you won't have connection issues during a live production. Wirecast Studio allows for up to two simultaneous Rendezvous guests, while Pro allows for up to seven.

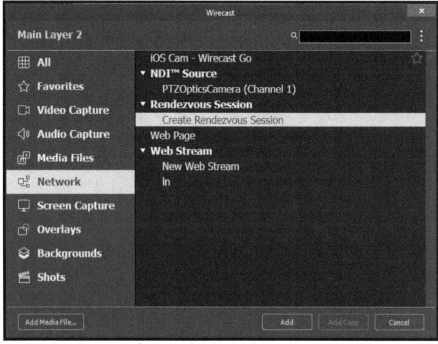

(Starting a Rendezvous Session to bring in remote callers)

Starting a Session

To initiate a Rendezvous session, add a new shot in the **Main Shot List** and choose **Create Rendezvous Session** under the **Network** category. This will open the **Rendezvous** dashboard. Once you have Rendezvous sessions setup, you can reconnect to a previous Rendezvous session here and add it as a shot.

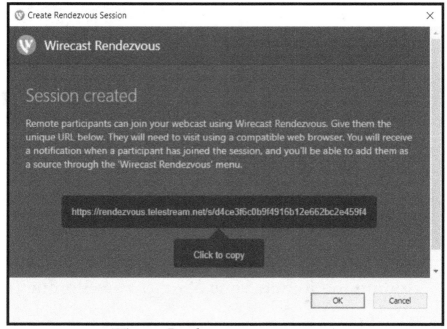

(Wirecast Rendezvous start up screen)

For a new session, copy the URL. This is what you will send to your participants to allow them to join. You can send that to the guest via email, text message, messaging app, or other communication channels. Next, hit OK to open the Rendezvous Dashboard.

Your guests can now access the link you sent in a web browser on a computer or their smart device. When your guest has entered their name and clicked Join, you will receive a notification that you can click to allow them to join.

(Wirecast Rendezvous Dashboard screen)

From the **Rendezvous Dashboard**, you can turn the guest's video on and off and mute their audio. You can also select the audio and video feed you would like your guests to see and hear, choosing one camera and up to two audio sources.

Adding the Rendezvous Shot to Your Production

Now, go back to the **Main Shot List**, add a new shot, and this time in the **Network** category, under **Rendezvous Session**, select your guest's name to add that person's audio and video as a shot.

Keep in mind that since your guests' audio and video can be added as a shot, they can also be used and manipulated as any other video source. You can set up a multi-layered picture-in-picture with multiple guests on the same screen, add titles and lower thirds and even place guests in boxes using virtual sets.

20 USING PLAYLISTS

Wirecast includes many features that allow you to set up parts of a live broadcast beforehand and allow those segments to run automatically when called upon. **Playlists** are a great way to bundle multimedia elements together to run during production. You can have multiple playlists, and you can edit them after they are created. You can even make changes as they are playing.

Creating Playlists

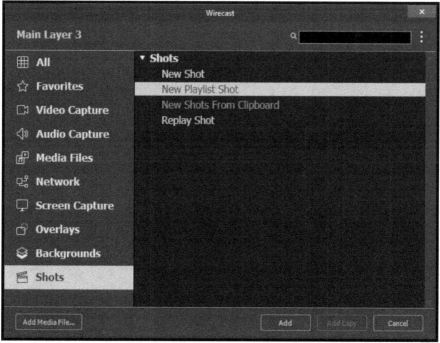

(Creating playlists in Wirecast)

There are two ways to create playlists in Wirecast. You can click the Plus (+) button in the **Main Shot List**, select the **Shots** category and then select **New Playlist Shot**. You can also simply drag an existing shot onto the top of another existing shot, and it will automatically create a new **Playlist** shot. You can continue to add shots to that **Playlist** by dragging and dropping.

(Wirecast Playlist tab)

You can edit any shot by double-clicking it to open the **Playlist Shot Editor**. Right-clicking on any shot in the **Playlist** will reveal different options than in the Main shot list. One important option is **Modifying Duration**.

Durations in Playlists

Playlists are designed to move automatically through the included shots. You can have great control of how and when transitions between shots happen. If you want the Playlist to play automatically, you will need to ensure that every shot has a duration. Pre-recorded video clips will have a duration. By default, it is set to the length of the clip.

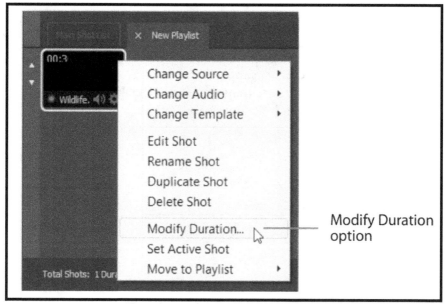

Modify Duration option

(Creating a duration for playlists)

For images and graphics, you will need to set the duration manually. Simply right-click on the clip and select Modify Duration. This will open the Shot Duration dialog box to set the time in hours, minutes, and seconds. If you have multiple clips that need durations, you can check the box to make this the default duration for the Playlist and click apply all to the current clips.

Live Shots

Live camera shots can be included in playlists. Keep in mind that live video has an infinite duration. So, if you want a transition to occur after a certain amount of time, you will need to set that clip's duration.

Editing and Manual Transitions

In the Playlist Shot editor, you can also adjust the transitions between clips using the same selection as offered in the main window. You can also manually advance to the next shot. You also have the option to set the behavior for when the Playlist is finished. You can choose to have it repeat, hold on the last slide, or transition the previous live shot, whatever is in the Preview window, or any other shot present in the same layer as your playlist.

Starting the Playlist

To get back to the Main Shot List, just click on the tab at the top of the panel. Once you are there, simply click on the Playlist to put it in Preview and then press the transition arrow to take it live. Once it is live, you will see countdown timers for both the current clip and the entire Playlist at the bottom of the program window.

21 MULTIVIEWER OUTPUT

Wirecast offers powerful **Multi-Viewer** support for your video production. This is especially helpful for complicated productions and situations where multiple operators are involved. With **Wirecast Studio**, Multi-Viewer output provides slots for up to four sources. With **Wirecast Pro**, there are available spaces for up to seventeen sources. Sources can be any view or shot. This includes **Preview**, **Program**, any shots from the **Main Shot List** including **Playlists**. The **Multi-Viewer** can be especially helpful to view live cameras to ensure they are ready to go live.

Setting Up Multi-Viewer

To set up the **Multi-Viewer** output, click on the small monitor icon at the bottom of the **Live** or **Preview** windows. This will open the **Multi-Viewer Configuration Window**. At the top of the window, you can select from your available monitors. After you choose the monitor, you can select the layout. Keep in mind that Wirecast Studio is limited to four slots. Next, you can choose whether or not to display labels for each shot and whether you want them below each shot or superimposed over them. Labels can be useful for identifying the shot, especially when using a layout with many sources.

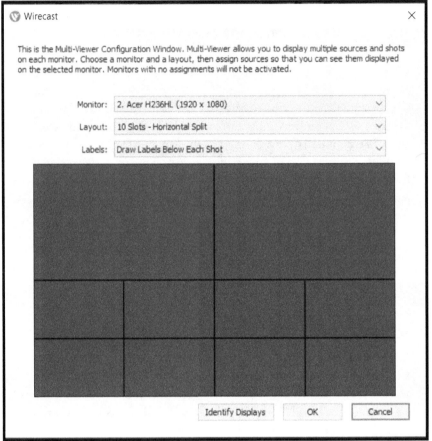

(Wirecast multiview setup options)

Assigning Shots

Now you can assign shots to each slot by simply clicking on the slot. At the top of the list, you will see that you can add both your **Live** and **Preview Windows**. Below that, you can add any shot that is in your **Main Shot List**. If you have additional monitors, you can return to the top of the configuration window and use the dropdown menu next to Monitor.

Once you have set up your **Multi-Viewer**, hitting **OK** will launch it. To exit the Multi-View at any time, use the escape key. You can always restart it using the Output dropdown menu, selecting **Multiple Viewer Output**, and clicking on the display you wish to start.

Keep in mind that, in addition to allowing you to view multiple shots on one monitor, you can also configure your monitor to display only one source. By turning off **Labels**, you can have a clean full-screen output of your Live or Preview monitor or any other shot. This can be an excellent solution for an additional output to a confidence monitor, projector, or screen in an overflow room.

22 ADDING OVERLAYS

With Wirecast's layering system, it is quick and easy to overlay additional text, images, or graphics to enrich your live production. Wirecast offers many options, including multiple ways of adding text, scoreboards, titles, and clocks, and timers.

To use overlays, it is essential to understand Wirecast's layering system. Since overlays like text do not take up the whole screen and have transparent backgrounds, they work well on the uppermost layers. That way, they are not obstructed by other shots.

To create an overlay, click the Plus (+) button to add a new shot and select the Overlays category on the left side.

Clock

To add a clock or timer, click Clock and then make adjustments in the Shot Manager Box's Clock Properties tab. You can name the clock, choose between a standard clock, countdown timer, or stopwatch, and set the look and feel. You can resize and reposition the clock in the frame as needed in the Preview window or the Shot Layer Properties tab.

Image Carousel

Image Carousels can rotate any number of images at preset durations. Simply select Image Carousel when adding a new shot. You can add your images and adjust the settings in the Image Carousel Properties box and drag to reposition the carousel in the Preview Window.

QR Code

This feature enables you to create an overlay of a QR code in just a couple of clicks. This is a great way to funnel online or in-person participants to a website linked to your even. Just add it as a shot and then add the content linked to the code to the Content box in the QR Code Generator Properties Box.

Scoreboard

For sporting events, Wirecast has several styles of built-in scoreboards. Once you have added a Scoreboard shot, you will find several custom options in the Scoreboard Properties box. You can name the scoreboard and choose the style. You can also decide if the scoreboard will have only scores or up to three additional information fields (such as quarter, period, down, fouls, etc.) There are several other customizable options for each scoreboard. This properties box is where you will adjust the score either manually or in intervals of one, two, or three points.

Text

The text overlay helps you add text in three main ways: manually, from a file, or an RSS feed. Once you have created the text shot, the Text Properties box gives you several formatting options and lets you choose where to pull the text from. You can simply type text in the box and, if necessary, change it on the fly throughout your production. You can also pull your text from a text (.txt) file. With this option, you can also select the option to keep reading the file. That means that someone else on a different computer on the same network could modify the file independently, with the changes showing up in Wirecast automatically. Text can also be pulled from an RSS (Really Simple Syndication) feed. RSS is a protocol for sharing web content as it is posted. This can be useful for sharing headlines, scores, or other updated information.

Titles

Wirecast has an extensive collection of title overlays, including title cards, lower thirds, boxes, and banners. These can be added just like any other shot, and text can be added to the graphics' preformatted areas in the Text Properties box.

23 ISO RECORDING AND REPLAY

ISO or isolated recording enables you to capture individual recordings of any live cameras connected to Wirecast. This means the entire feed will be recorded even if that camera is not in the Live Window. This is useful for post-production purposes or for creating live replays during sporting events and other live activities.

(Wirecast ISO recording notification button)

Configuring ISO Recording

To configure ISO recording, use the Replay+ISO dropdown of the main menu and select Configure. This will open the dialogue boxes that will allow you to add and manage ISO cameras. Clicking the Plus (+) button or the Add ISO button opens the configuration menu. There you can name the recording for later reference. Choose the source from the dropdown below. Keep in mind that only physically connected devices will be available. This includes cameras, capture cards, microphones, and audio interfaces. If your intended source is greyed out in the dropdown, you will need to exit out of this menu and add that device as a shot in the main shot menu before proceeding.

Under Audio Source, use the dropdown menu to choose among available sources. In some situations, you may want to capture audio that comes with the video source. This would be appropriate if the source is a camera with a built-in or external microphone. In other cases, you may wish to capture audio from another source, such as an audio interface.

Next, you can set your recording quality. Keep in mind that if you are recording your main output feed and multiple ISO feeds, you will be using considerable storage space. Double-check your storage capacity before deciding on a quality level. Now you can choose your filename and the destination folder for recording.

If you are recording ISO to make use of the replay feature, check the Configure this ISO for Replay box. If not, you can choose whether to record all to one file or split files at a predetermined length.

For ISO recording made for replay, you can now set up keyboard shortcuts to create, update, or mark this replay. On the Output List on the left side of the configuration box, you can click Replay Settings. This provides control for the behavior of replays, including default and maximum duration and what you wish to happen once the replay is created. These are important since they will impact how your replay system works.

For instance, the default duration will determine how far back in the recording the system will save once you create your replay. For example, if the default duration is set to 30 seconds, when you create a replay shot, it will capture the 30 seconds before the moment you issue the command.

The "Create Replays In" dropdown allows you to determine where the replay clip will be placed when created. You can also choose to automatically place the shot in Preview, where you can edit the clip's duration, speed, and magnification before sending it to the Live window.

24 HOTKEYS

Hotkeys are the perfect tool for streaming your live video productions, enabling you to switch to particular shots with just the touch of a button.

To access the **Hotkey Manager,** you can either right-click on an existing shot, choose **Keyboard Shortcut** and click manage. Or, open the main preferences menu and select the **Keyboard Shortcuts** tab. From this dialogue box, you can add and remove shortcuts using the plus (+) and minus (-) buttons.

To set up, a new hotkey hit the Plus (**+**) button. First, give it a name. You can just name it as the key you will use to activate the shortcut. However, to better keep track of various shortcuts, it may be better to give it a more defined title. Next, press **"click to record shortcut."** The software will wait for you to press the key or key combination you wish to use. Key combinations can include standard keys plus alternate keys such as shift, command, control, etc. If you choose a key combination already in use by the software, you will receive an error. Otherwise, your shortcut has been created.

To assign a shortcut, just right click on any shot, go to **Keyboard Shortcut** and click on the hotkey you created. The shortcut will appear in the thumbnail image of the shot. Keep in mind that hotkeys can be assigned to multiple shots as long as they are on different layers. So, for instance, you wanted to add a clock overlay, a scoreboard, and some text, you could assign one key to activate all three.

For even faster access to shots, hotkeys can be combined with the AutoLive feature. With AutoLive off, pressing a shortcut key will only put the attached shot or shots into the preview window. If, however, you want the hotkey to send a shot or shots directly to the Live window, you can activate **AutoLive**. Simply go to the Switch menu and click on AutoLive. You can turn **AutoLive** off at any time by returning to that menu. You can also toggle it on and off using Command-I on a Mac or Control-I on a PC.

25 CONCLUSION

Video production is a powerful field of study that enables you to tell a visual story. Visual stories have become a primary way to communicate online today. A software solution like Wirecast is special because it allows you to connect your storytelling capabilities with online audiences. Growth in online communications driven by social media websites such as Facebook and YouTube have made production software an invaluable tool for modern communications.

Over my years in the video production industry, I have learned that our industry is full of wonderful people. I encourage you to join the StreamGeeks Facebook group and share the projects you are working on. Feel free to ask for help and you may be surprised how willing the community is to help.

You can supplement your learning with the online Udemy course available with this book. You can learn more about this course at https://www.udemy.com/course/wirecast-training.

Also, feel free to email me directly if you have any questions.

Paul Richards
Chief Streaming Officer
StreamGeeks
paul.richards@streamgeeks.us

ABOUT THE AUTHOR

Paul Richards is a father, an author, and a business executive leading his company in the exciting field of video communications. Richards is the author of multiple top-selling books that draw from his hands-on experience in the audio visual technology industry. As the Director of Business Development for HuddleCamHD and PTZOptics, Richards is the host of multiple online shows that feature his work on YouTube, Facebook, LinkedIn and Twitch. Richards is the author of "The Virtual Ticket," "The Online Meeting Survival Guide" and "Helping Your Church Live Stream."

Paul is also the Chief Streaming Officer at StreamGeeks and where he teaches online Udemy courses for over 45,000 students. His courses cover subjects such as live video production, online communications and social media connectivity.

GLOSSARY OF TERMS

3.5mm Audio Cable: Male to male stereo cable, common in standard audio uses.

4K: A high definition resolution option (3840 x 2160 pixels or 4096 x 2160 pixels)

API [Application Program Interface]: A streaming API is a set of data a social media network uses to transmit on the web in real time. Going live directly from YouTube or Facebook login uses their API.

Bandwidth - The range of frequencies within a given band, in particular that used for transmitting a signal.

Broadcasting - The distribution of audio or video content to a dispersed audience via any electronic mass communications medium.

Broadcast Frame Rates - Used to describe how many frames per second are captured in broadcasting. Common frame rates in broadcast include: **29.97fps and 59.97 fps.**

Capture Card - A device with inputs and outputs that allow a camera to connect to a computer.

Chroma Key - A video effect that allows you to layer images and manipulate color hues [i.e. green screen]

Cloud Based Streaming - Streaming and video production interaction that occurs within the cloud, therefore accessible beyond a single user's computer device.

Color Matching - The process of managing color and lighting settings on multiple cameras to match their appearance.

Community Strategy - The strategy of building one's brand and product recognition by building meaningful relationships with an audience, partner, and clientele base.

Content Delivery Network [CDN] - A network of servers that deliver web based content to an end user.

CPU [Central Processing Unit] Usage - the electronic circuitry within a computer that carries out the instructions of a computer program by performing the basic arithmetic, logical, control and input/output (I/O) operations specified by the instructions.

DAW - Digital Audio Workstation.

DB9 Cable - A common cable connection for camera joystick serial control.

DHCP [Dynamic Host Configuration Protocol] Router - A router with a network management protocol that dynamically sets IP addresses so the server can communicate with its sources.

Encoder - A device or software that converts a piece of code or info to then distribute it.

H.264 & H.265 - Common formats of video recording, compression, and delivery.

HDMI [High Definition Multimedia Interface] - A cable commonly used for transmitting audio/video.

HEVC [High Efficiency Video Coding] - H.264, one of the most common formats of video, MJPEG-H Part 2.

IP [Internet Protocol] Camera/Video - A camera or video source that can send and receive information via a network & internet.

IP Control - The ability to control/connect a camera or device via a network or internet.

Latency - The time it takes between sending a signal and the recipient receiving it. [more]

Live Streaming - The process of sending and receiving audio and or video over the internet.

LAN [Local Area Network] - A network of computers linked together in one location.

Multicorder - A feature of streaming software that allows the user to record raw footage or a camera feed to a file separate from the stream output. [more]

NDI® [Network Device Interface] - Software standard developed by NewTek to enable video-compatible products to communicate, deliver, and receive broadcast quality video in a high quality, low latency manner that is frame-accurate and suitable for switching in a live production environment.

NDI® Camera - A camera that allows you to send and receive video over your LAN.

NDI®|HX — NDI® High Efficiency, optimizes NDI® for limited bandwidth environments.

Network - A digital telecommunications network which allows nodes to share resources. In computer networks, computing devices exchange data with each other using connections between nodes.

NTSC - Video standard used in North America.

OTT Streaming [Over-The-Top] - When a media service bypasses typical media distributors (ie. Facebook, YouTube, Twitch) to distribute content.

PAL - Analog video format commonly used outside of North America.

PCIe Card - Allows high bandwidth communication between a device and the computer's motherboard.

PoE - Power over ethernet.

PTZ - Pan, tilt, zoom.

RS-232 - Serial camera control transmission.

RTMP [Real Time Messaging Protocol] -

RTSP [Real Time Streaming Protocol] - Network control protocol for streaming from one point to point.

Introducing The Unofficial Guide to Wirecast.

This book an invaluable resource for Wirecast users new and old. With over 20 chapters of detailed technical writing, author Paul Richards, has included time saving tips that increase your production value and your proficiency with Wirecast software.

If you plan to use Wirecast for professional video production, this book is for you.

www.ingramcontent.com/pod-product-compliance
Lightning Source LLC
LaVergne TN
LVHW051712050326
832903LV00032B/4156